Moon Dreams
Coloring Books For Adults Relaxation

Sonya Cowan

Moon Dreams
Coloring Books For Adults Relaxation

Copyright: Published in the United States by **Sonya Cowan**

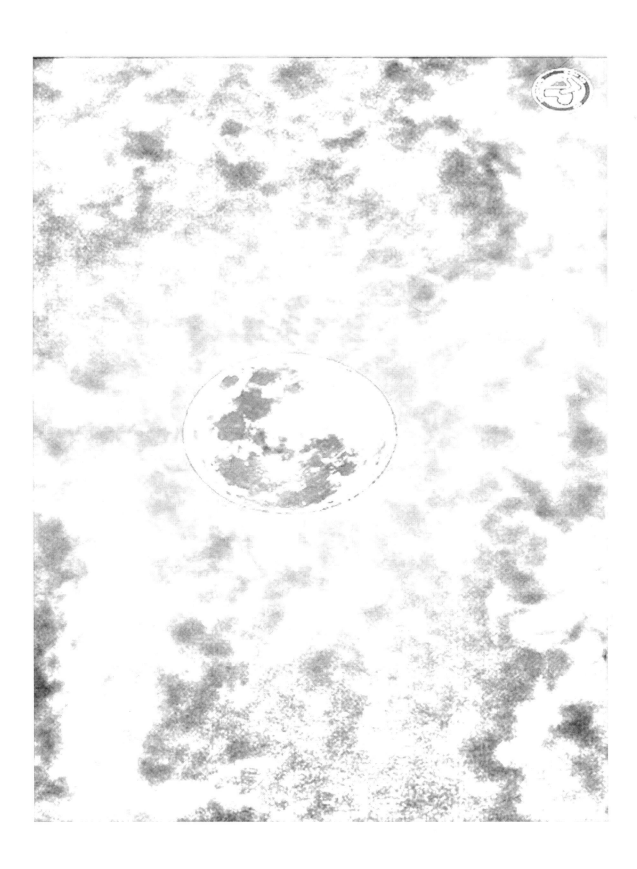

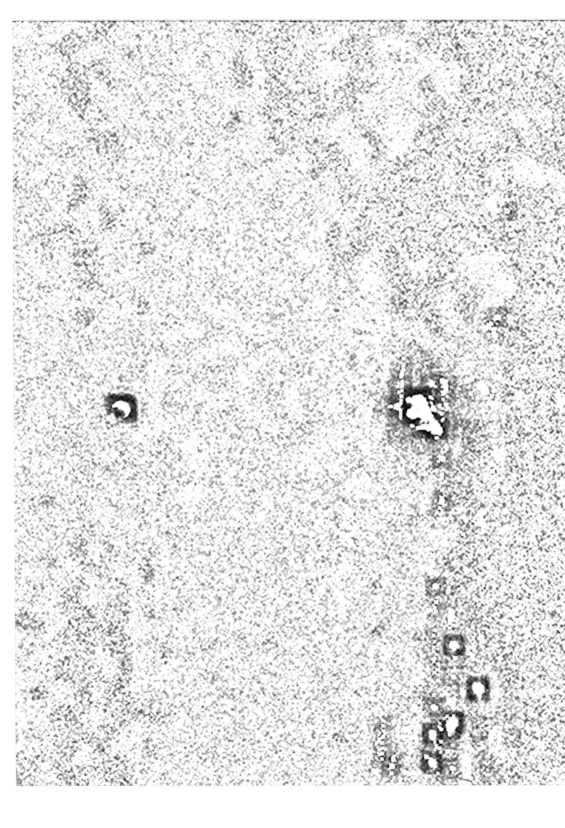

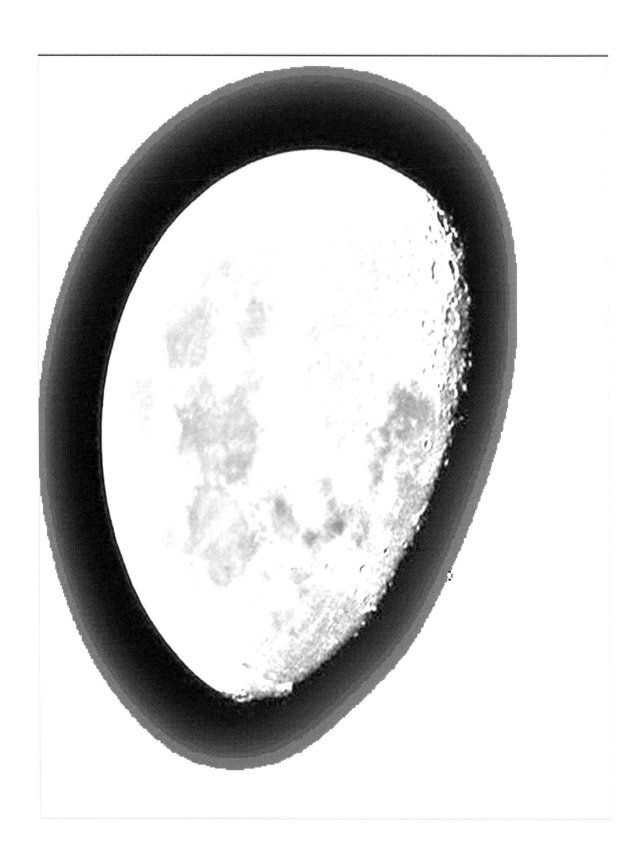

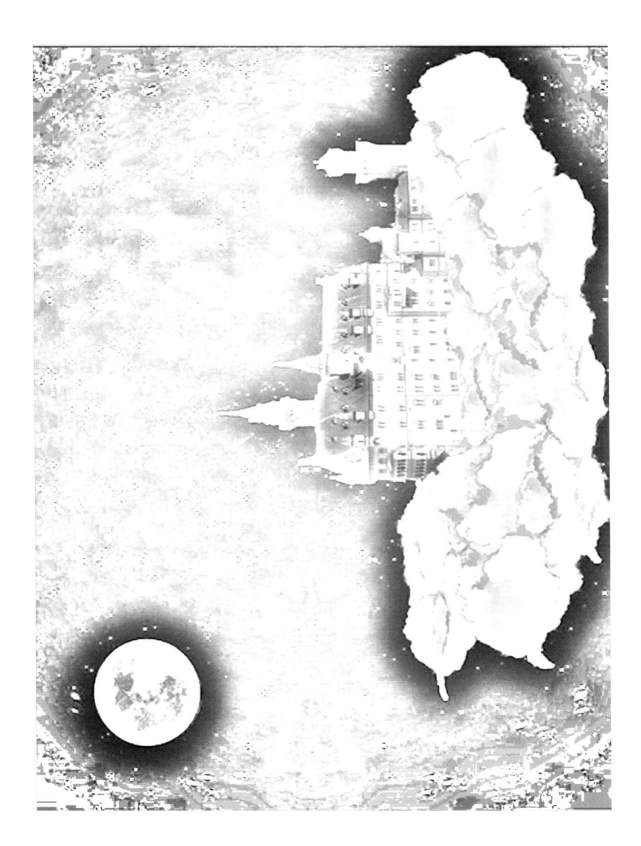

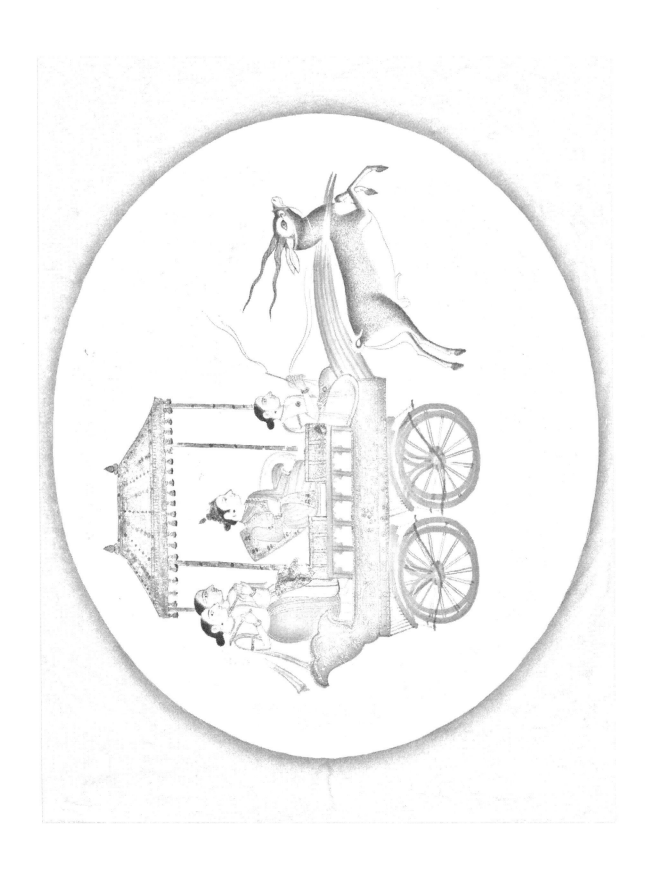

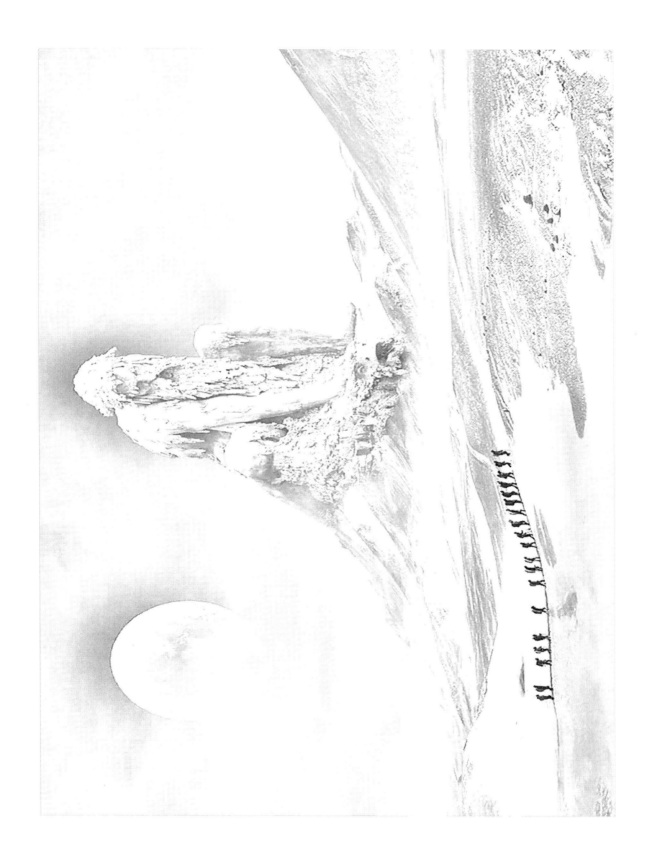

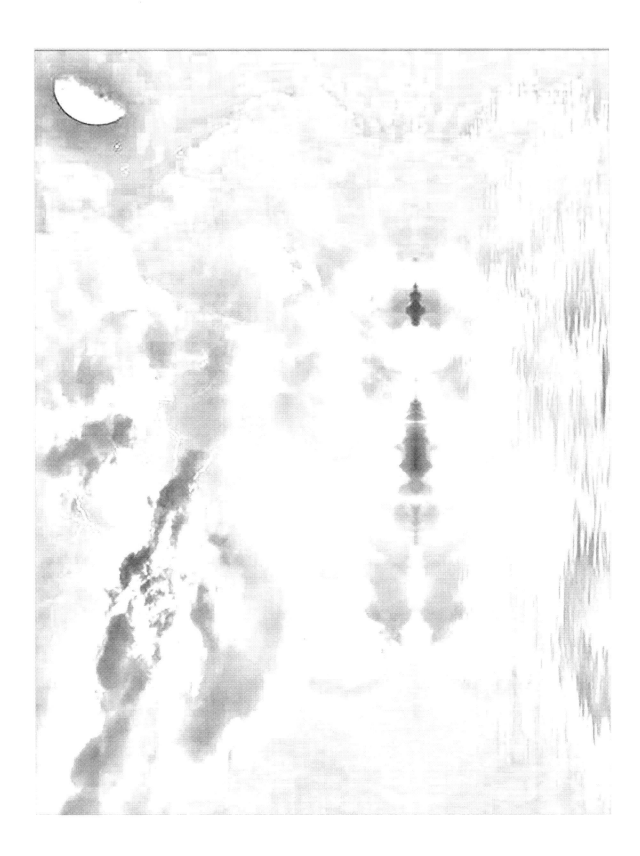

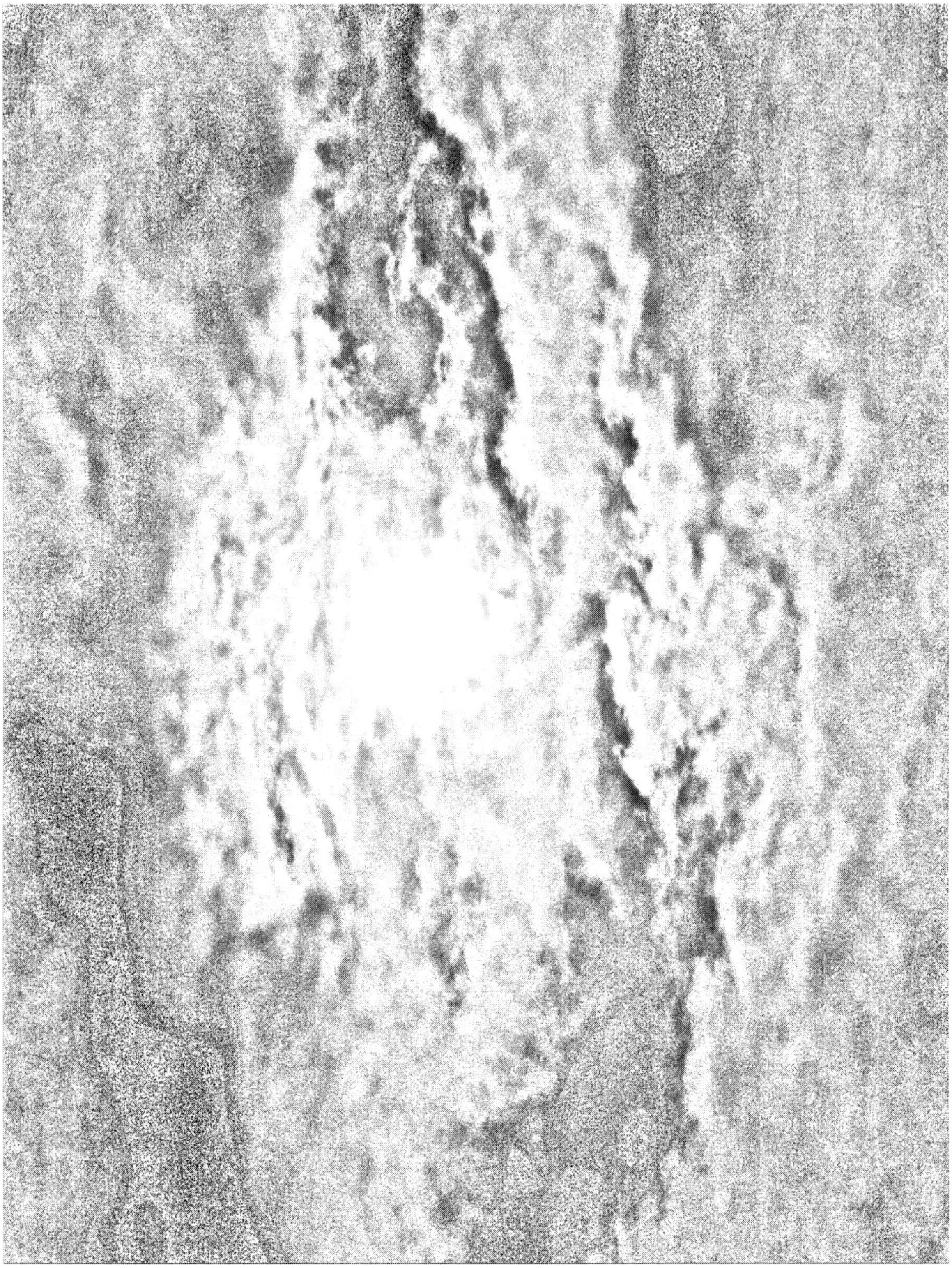

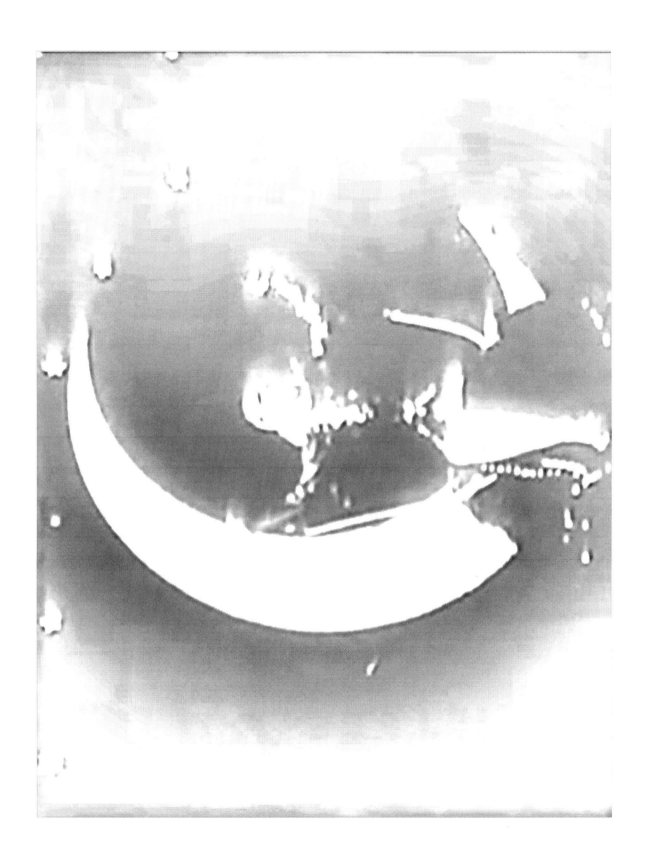

midatlantic union of
vietnamese student associations
presents its first annual charity ball.s

a bless dream

{a black tie event}

come celebrate with MAUVSA a year's worth of fundraising for VOICE.

VOICE (Vietnamese ... Initiative for Conscience Empowerment) is a non-profit organization; providing a voice for the ... Vietnamese community through education and advocacy for the protection of Vietnamese women and children in South-east-Asia and other ... of Vietnamese refugees, con... confronting the conscience of our community

when:
saturday, june 7, 2008
8:00 pm - 12:00 am

where:
9630 gudelsky drive, rockville, MD 20:
shuttle provided from shady grove metro from 7:30

how much:
for advance sales: $20 a couple, $15 single
at the door: $15 per person
for tickets, please contact mauvsa@gmail.com

{light refreshments will be provided}

MAUVSA
www.mauvsa.org

VOiCE

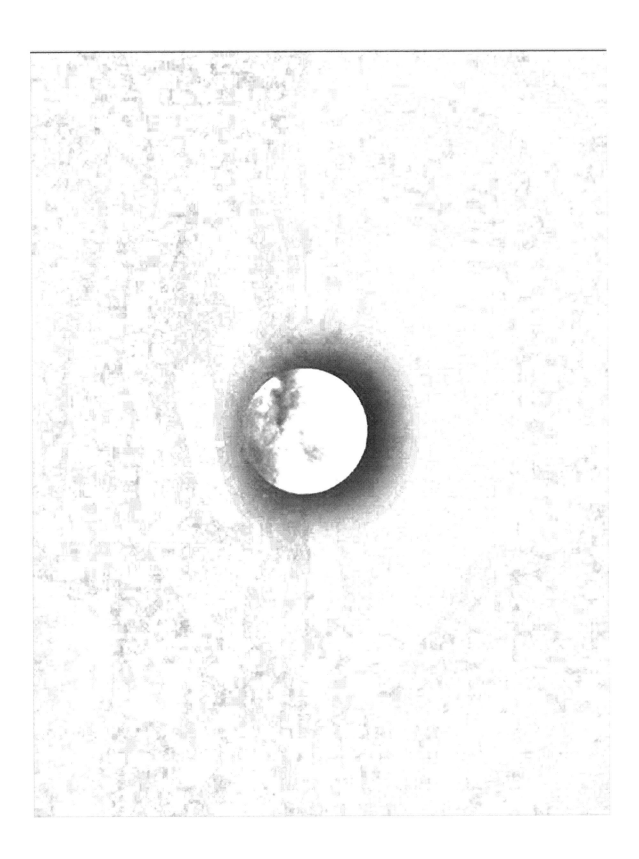

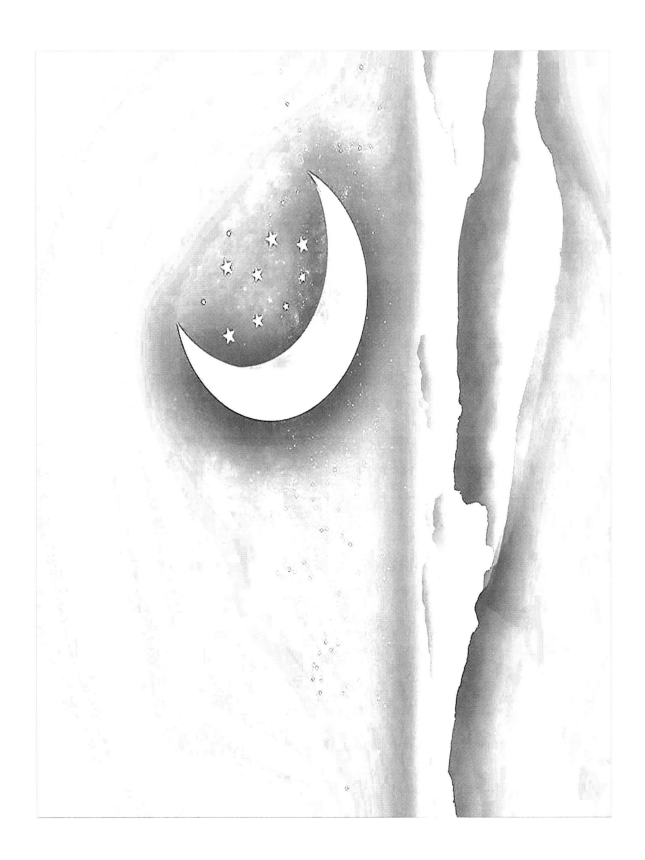

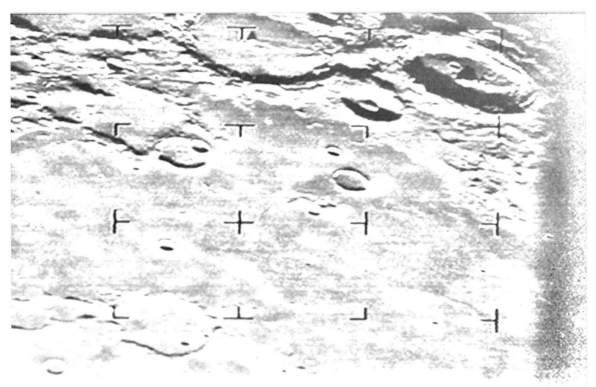

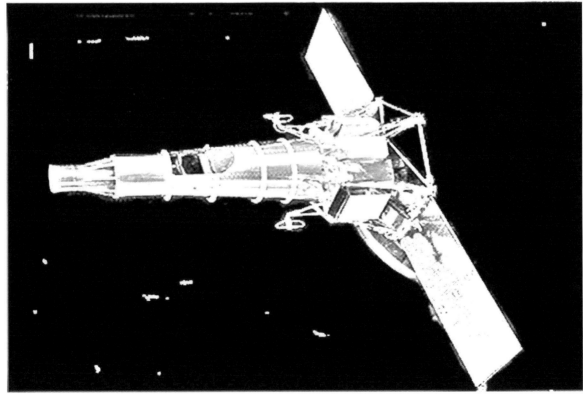

Thank you

Made in the USA
Monee, IL
20 March 2022

93168981R00059